Post-Catholic Midrashim

poems by

Karina Lutz

Finishing Line Press
Georgetown, Kentucky

Post-Catholic Midrashim

*To the memory of my mother,
Carol Ruth Lombard Lutz*

Copyright © 2019 by Karina Lutz
ISBN 978-1-64662-064-7 First Edition
All rights reserved under International and Pan-American Copyright Conventions. No part of this book may be reproduced in any manner whatsoever without written permission from the publisher, except in the case of brief quotations embodied in critical articles and reviews.

ACKNOWLEDGMENTS

"Ash and light," *Tulane Review* (Spring 2015): 7.

"Dear Emily," *Wilderness House Press 41* 11.1 (Spring 2016).

"Grace after sex," For Women Who Roar *Volume 1: LGBTQ Pride Poems* (July 2019).

"Locus of control," *the RavensPerch* (June 5, 2016).

"May the child be at peace," *Narrative Northeast* (Jan. 3, 2016).

"The bitterness of the ancestresses/spit upon me," *Incandescent Mind* II (Winter 2017).

"Who," *Buddhist Poetry Review* X (Fall 2013).

Publisher: Leah Maines
Editor: Christen Kincaid
Cover Art: Hannah Lutz Winkler
Author Photo: Bobbie Hunger
Cover Design: Elizabeth Maines McCleavy

Printed in the USA on acid-free paper.
Order online: www.finishinglinepress.com
also available on amazon.com

Author inquiries and mail orders:
Finishing Line Press
P. O. Box 1626
Georgetown, Kentucky 40324
U. S. A.

Table of Contents

Introduction ix

Parable of the parabola 1

Suicidal Catholic 4

The bitterness of the ancestresses
    spit upon me 5

Grace after sex 7

Into your hands I commend my spirit 8

Easter gathering 10

May the child be at peace 11

Dear Emily 12

Anticipating the *Akedah* moment 13

Ash Wednesday 14

What a fragile earth it is without a God.
    What a violent one it is with one. 16

Amniotic stage of the [n]ew [a]ge 17

Locus of control 20

Who 21

Ash and light 22

Suicidal Buddha 23

I am therefore I am whatever 24

Today, the usual 25

Transcendence/immanence 27

To be one of wisdom's guests 28

[coda] Touching the Earth 29

Introduction

Midrashim are Judaic interpretations of scriptures, which often elaborate the stories found only in skeleton form there. In this spirit, contrary to the ways of Catholic dogma, I interrogate the social-spiritual effects of historic Catholic interpretations, including a child's mind's understanding. My parents raised me what I call "social-justice Catholic." In contrast to the better-known right wing of Catholicism, this vein's moral imperatives were to rectify inequality and end war, at least during the period I was brought up. Those values are integral to how I have moved in the world. At the same time, it took years of inquiry and vigilance—and yes, even prayer—to disentangle myself from the Church's more insidious patriarchal and punitive thought systems and contradictions. Forty-four years after leaving the Church, I keep having to extract and reinterrogate what hides in the early-formed folds of my brain. Therefore these poems: *Post-Catholic Midrashim*.

Careening between sass and earnestness, the poems rail against religion, while struggling to recover an authentic spirituality. I debate my late mother's theology, at the same time as I try to honor her truth, her own questioning, her extraordinary intelligence, and her ability to live with/in the contradictions. I don't so much argue with God as I argue against religions' big lies.

Perhaps every religion places big lies next to the big truths, where the lies shine like moons through no light of their own.

Parable of the parabola

Judas and Pilate push the rock but
realize the tomb's in a hollow
and it's all uphill from there.

The greatest heist of all, perhaps,
but was it planned?
Or remorse?

On this rock hope of an afterlife is built.

They push, and push, and finally
can hear Jesus's voice, human
as anything. I surmise
it was Pilate's remorse
                          and Judas's plot.
But I only had the gospels
according to Caesar (being Roman
Catholic by a long tradition of quasi-accidental birth)
'though I took First Holy Communion the day after Vatican II
whisked away the old catechism (meaning day in the Genesisian sense,
which carbon dating puts at *epoch*)
(and meaning *Communion* in the sense of *grave
disappointment when the plasticky poprock wafer
sank into the surface tension of the slick of saliva on my tongue
and yet did nothing to my already alienated seven-year-old heart,*

*which to this day droops with hope of dissolving all culturally induced separation,
peyote to the tongue, psilocybin to the tongue, clitoris and glans to tongue
notwithstanding.*

Still, I yearn to live that promised life
in the no man's land of America,
by which I mean I walk over the body and blood
of the ancestors of this land
but they are not my ancestors.

I hear only echoes, unable to tell
which mountains reflect, which reverberate, and which
are speaking to me...
Okay, sorry, settlers' worries, it's not that bad.). That is to say,
I had only the Emperor's side of the story

1

until I grew up and read the Gospel of Mary Magdalene and *wow*.

I know, I know, I left Pilate and Judas at the rock.
So. Jesus's eyes have adapted to the crack of light
and he's heard who it is out there.
The crescent of sunlight falling on the back wall of the tomb
said "Good morning!" and he has his divine sleeping roll
rolled up and is ready to rock
and he helps with the pushing at a hopeful angle—
as little as he can visualize
what's happening out there, what with
the two grown men bickering about "how"
like boys over a stickball game.

Passion for justice for his people
—the uber-last temptation—arises as
aim at Pilate, who he might not yet realize
is in on the plot.

Jesus knew his part—turn a cheek to a kiss
—toss a table and a token—coin a phrase or two—
carry the cross willfully—or was *that* his mistake,
failure to stick with the civil disobedience discipline of staying *put*—

as if one can force a condemned man to do anything,
as if a proven miracle worker
who is planning to ascend
would ever fear death.

"Turn the other cheek *away*!" I yell,
but history carries voices only one direction,
like TV used to, when we learned
the freedom of yelling at it
when a president called for war,
for example, and mentioned God
in the same speech, as if.
Back then we basked in the inconsequentiality of our yelling:
no president could hear, no secret police,
no Siri, just the original Sirius,
no meta-analysis of Alexa,
no Big Data, just Big Daddy in the sky able to see,

who might appreciate,
or not...

So there's Jesus, like I said, pushing,
with, at, or against Pilate and/or Judas (they cannot see)
and here I am, wondering when
communion will be real and constant,
and the rock moves
and they all take off
and the Women come
and wonder when they see Him on the road
what really happened
and can't count on a straight answer

as all turns parabolic,
the rock at the vertex.

Suicidal Catholic

To imagine why she needed her stomach pumped
was to imagine a pain greater than the fear of hell,
not the kind of thing a child is used to.
It was to imagine hating so hard
you'd fill your own mouth with acid
just to be able to spit it
at a universe too evil to stop the pain
and too cold to reveal
its purpose.

It seemed no one else would imagine this,
not even her.
So I did it for her.
Did it for all of them.

**The bitterness of the ancestresses
spit upon me**

What did I do wrong?
my child-self wanted to know
Nothing but to exist
to be hers
                      out of her body in spite
                            of herself
                    to spite perhaps
     her love
   her love of sex, surely
her *pulchritude*, my dad would call it
in us,
her unwanted daughters.

In age and decrepitude
my mother has finally had enough
of so much,
finally heard enough:

It was her own monsignor,
in the end, implicated,
pimping his own parish,
who prompted her to turn her back
on the church,

which means she faced me now

as she began to make comedic confessions
to anyone:

"Bless me Father, for I have sinned...
I think...maybe...
I wasn't supposed to have all these children?"
and she laughs her demented laugh
now that dementia frees her mind.
"Do you know what it's like, Father?"
and she laughs hysterically
in spite of the hysterectomy.

Not just in spite, *to* spite.
She spits the bitterness

of our ancestresses.
I dodge
like only an abused child knows how:
standing a little narrow—
one hip back—
the little twist in the spine
to be ready to spring.

Then, in the end, safe.
Then, curious.
Light-years from their passing,
I ask her about these women:
We pore over the sepia and silver prints
the black paper corners loosening.

This, dear reader,
is unfathomable progress from the arguments
we used to have about whether abortion
is moral, which always ended: "If *I*
believed in abortion
you wouldn't exist."

I'd laugh: *inconceivable!*

Grace after sex

The only sign that lovers had been there
was a clean set of sheets and two towels in the dryer.
Two mugs in the dish drainer
could have been her and her husband's from their last visit.
Anything new in the air did not have a scent
separable from the scent of this place:
gulls' middens, tides' expositions,
and wind-sprayed salt spritz.
The wastebaskets were empty.
Yet she knew, just below awareness,
for her friends' prayer loitered in the place:

"Glorious goddess: creator of these spirited bodies
and their lovemaking—
creator of forces as gentle and powerful
as snowflakes and earthquakes—
thank you.

"And thank you for the rubber tree,
who lets us love many this way."

Into your hands I commend my spirit

"My God, my God, why have you forsaken me?"

"Forsaken?" replied His Father, "Who carried this cross here, upon which you hang?"

"I was forced," Jesus hung his head.

His Father questioned: "Knowing you were to face down death, you allowed them to *force* you?
What were you afraid of?"

Silence.

"You once said it, my son:
give to Caesar what is Caesar's."

"I guess I didn't know all I meant.
I see I could have resisted their control every step."

"Yes, not the time to *turn the other cheek.*
To turn the first cheek, *sans* cooperation,
would have been enough. Don't give them the pleasure,
just their reflections."

"I guess I was caught up in the passion of it all."

"Yes, my love, you took it and ran."

"And here I hang, in agony,"
and agony lifted, and peace descended.

* * *

"Miracle boy." Father again.

"Yes?"

"Do not allow anyone to enslave you.
Teach them that."

"By dying."

"This time, by dying."

"And next time?"

"*When we are firmly established in nonviolence, all beings around us cease to feel hostility.[1]*"

"I've seen that done."

"You have done it."

"So I have taught it."

"But you lost your groove."

"So here I am."

"Having forsaken yourself, ourSelf…
…temporarily."

"Ah.

"*It is done.*"

---

1 Patanjali, *Yoga Sutras*, trans. Alistair Shearer

Easter gathering

The children scrambled, looking for plastic eggs
filled with wrapped candies:
What is hidden! What is inside!

One child climbed a tree and found
an empty nest made of last year's grass and mud,
the inside smooth and curved as if made on a potter's wheel.

Parents smile at the child's vestigial skill,
her limbs braided with branches,
call her *"our little monkey."*

She rubs her hand across the mud, imagines
a world where the eggs are there, the eggs are real.

Might we call her *human*?

Looking down, empty-
handed, she asks,
"Mom, what is *eternal*?

May the child be at peace

May the child be at peace.
May the child's peace radiate to all in her grasp.
May the child's peace radiate to all whose grasp she is within.
May the pedophile be at peace,
and the pimp and the coyote be at peace.

May the child soldiers' commander be at peace.
May the commander's arms dealer be at peace
and the arms maker
and the investor
and the pensioner
and the inventor of money.

And you and I, my friends, and you and I.

Dear Emily

Maybe 'eternity'
is simply a very long time—
useful hyperbole
meaning we suspend
belief in winter long enough
to not disquiet summer,

to ungird, to not dread,
to not believe
the dead are dead.

Anticipating the *Akedah* moment

May I listen for truth
the critical moments between emptiness and idea
between idea and choice
between choice and doing
between doing and continuing to do—
each machination of manifestation
all along the continuum of creation
in awe of the known and the unknown:
Amen.

Ash Wednesday

"Suffer us not to mock ourselves with falsehood." —T.S. Eliot

Mom, you taught me to give up my pillow for Lent.
The crick in my neck a question mark:
Why are we meant to create new pain to transcend?
So much already braces this world against itself:
hurt people hurting people, children killing children,
all of us neglecting our loves
as we indulge in our own suffering,
and heaping more suffering upon that
in confusion over the glimmer of truth under those bushels:

that to acknowledge pain may redeem us.

To acknowledge, not to create: to be with what is, bearing lightly.
For life is suffering, and life is good.

For my last Lent, once old enough, I gave up
the belief that we need to resist our harmless comforts.
And I put down the cross,
snapped open *that* crick in my shoulder;
I could finally start to unsnarl my spine.

I found a different way to renounce
selfishness, found the best things to give up to be
the beliefs that bind and blind.

So when I called you, Mom, and you told me
this Ash Wednesday you were renouncing
only what harms,
joy poured through me
like warm rain through snow,
like this day, the break of spring!

Before my ears, you dumped bushels of stored suffering
you'd saved for this transformative day,
for this transformative season
when sky and earth
grumble towards, burst towards each other,

Joy pours to you as you trade your leeching pain
for the creaking open,
the floating down that is healing,
the splitting open like fully ripe fruit
that is healing.

So the old church crashes down around us,
and we stand and gaze unhurt
at the naked sky,
its splendor,
its silence.

May a few of these temple pillars remain,
sacred ruins,
later to point us back toward this light.

Here, love who made me,
rest your head on the pillow.
To give up is not to suffer
if we give up the causes of our suffering.

The test is joy.

What a fragile earth it is without a God.
What a violent one it is with one.

Both camps, those who see only one God, far above,
and those who see only Earth,
project their particular fragility and wrath.

For Cartesian ecologists, earth's movements are just facts of physics
and all its life is as tenuous as a hypothesis;
nothing like the world of Noah,
as he mourned over the side of the ark
(tears abetting the rising sea).

Wrath:

for if God is all-powerful and perfect, and we, the sinners,
then these floods, droughts, and quakes must be
His intent to harm us.

Fragility:

for if no One holds the intention to keep this ecology together,
and we oafish humans keep stomping through, trampling rare species
without feeling a thing through our thick rubber soles,

then earth's elegant creation is but an exquisite accident.
Our own evolution appears as the fatal flaw
to undo all life's intricacies,

as if entropy trumps order every time,
as if order is not the very nature of chaos,
as if there could be no intelligence greater than our own,
       no creativity inherent in being…

No doubt Noah did a little science on the sly:
taxonomy a perk of fulfilling the command.
And no doubt an unconscious faith keeps
scientists afloat as they count new species,
still not having found two of everything.

(Or our tears would again abet the rising seas.)

Amniotic stage of the [n]ew [a]ge

Back in the 'seventies, for lack of a spiritual life,
we imagined one,
went through new motions
(picture: tai chi done without grace);
climbed mountains chattering incessantly
(like city squirrels on a resort holiday);
or in all sincerity sought spirit,
if not from moment to moment,
from time to time.

We took tiny tabs of windowpane for a bigger view:
or swallowed whole
some kind of Ecstasy precursor:
$5 or less for a quantum leap.
All the while, somehow, we avoided or despaired or grieved the
ultimate
        Reality
                we craved.

Before it became a marketing category, and was [C]apitalized,
'new age' meant a smorgasbord of eclectic pieces of practices,
a syncretic smattering, a veritable stockpile of spirit,
and we rode the paroxysms of the stock market of our core greed:
                our hungriest loneliness
and the gall/the blister/the cocoon we built against emptiness;
meanwhile exquisite emptiness remained, holed up inside
each moment.

Some of us happily left the label behind;
just as it was going from unorganized religion
to marketing category, we left the [n]ew [a]ge behind.
We saw through the reactionary
passivity of believing *time will deliver*. Or saw numbers
of astrologically divined deadlines pass without peace
descending as foreseen;
saw wannabe prophets washed up like fourth-rate economists
who never hit the jackpot of prediction.

Or, encountering one too many create-your-own-reality-
checks–like that one last *soi-disant* creator creating

his own bliss at our expense, and blaming
us for the consequence–
we might have recognized the pattern
of patriarchy, discerned the cast of caste.

For my friends and me, it was the day we shuffled into the apartment
of a channeler in LA (where coincidentally live a lot of unemployed actors)
who told us the Jews were in on the holocaust's
planning, before birth. "We all choose our parents," he said,
"And the Jews and Germans agreed from the spirit realm
to create that reality."

Like any religion, this one (fitfully forming) held great truths
next to big lies
               where a glow might reflect or refract,
                                           or distract
like the lesser lights of the bardos,
or Narnia's Turkish delight,
like Mara, or Milarepa's caveful of demons,
or the partial illumination of the Tarot's Moon.

Still, of all those poses, prayers, and practices
something couldn't help helping:
offering glimpses, terrors, fractured moments of being engulfed
in purification, or worse,
in nothing.

In space, without a spacesuit.

Or peace might pierce our pomposity,
glimmer a light greater than grandiosity.

Years later, we've come to embrace nothing again: we seek emptiness
to salve the commotion;
of course, at first it seems to be nowhere to be found!
The threat of awakening is still a dream
the memory of which starts
at the end when we can't find our clothes after skinny dipping—

and we wake up to this life wishing we could remember
the warm water on our skin before the cold air—

remember being dressed in translucence—
remember
that we are sleeping snug
in the purity of what we are made of
before we are made—

Who knew
it was this brilliant light
had blinded us?

Who knew
emptiness is the medium
of all light?

Even in the amniotic stage,
we knew.
And
we know we have yet to know.

Illusion persists
                                      yet
                                     truth
                                     just
                                      is.

Locus of control

My mother and I stepped over trash
        on a sidewalk, and she taught me
        to judge the litterers.

My father taught me
        to pick it up: the glee of superiority.

My priest and our youth group
        stepped around a drunk face down
        on a sidewalk, and he taught us
        selective ministry.

My government and my peace group
        debated the war and then
        how to leave, what is our
        duty,
        who it is
        who has the moral authority to take
        responsibility
        for the mess we have made.

Who do we think we are?
Who do we think we are?

Who

Cupped hands hold ashes
up to wind.
Lighter than sand,
heavier
than feathers,

the ashes
    stream,
        billow,
            drift.

Grey clouds
already plump with smoke
    embrace,
        absorb,
            carry
back to life's realms.
    air,
        water,
            soil,
reinhume, while the humans
wait to inhale, then do.

Drop to knees and place
what remains, grit of bone,
in the fire circle,
now cold, still ready.

Ash and light

Dependently coarising:
body and mind.
Independently falling apart:
two halves of a coconut
roll away from each other.
The machete hovers and withdraws.

The match burned out.
Or did the flame
burn through the match?

What is left? Everything,
some as light (some as ash)
across the universe.

Suicidal Buddha

> *"Abandon any hope of fruition."* —a Tibetan lojong precept

This many-petaled lotus likes
to pluck itself: seeking what is enclosed
by destroying enclosure: seeking the core
of space at the center as if
it is not formed by those very petals,
as if when the plucked petals float to the ground
they disappear or are forgotten,
as if holding
can be done without hands,
as if the beauty of that curved space
at the center is not blooming,
is not what blooming is.

[coda]

As if a petal thus plucked
dissolves into space
like a thought
   uncaptured
      unremembered
         unfinished

I am therefore I am whatever

I am a leaf in the forest
deep in the understory
back when there was a canopy.
I am waiting for the angle of the sun
wherein is my moment
                to receive
                to glint white (as seen from above)
                to shine gold-edged green (as seen from below)

(if you are bird or squirrel flying or climbing above and below)
for you to see both.

I am cell-wide sunfilled (to be seen through).

I imagine therefore I am

and you.

Today, the usual

I.
What of your walk today will you remember?
No great blue heron fished in the reeds, through the ice,
like that day last winter.

You saw no friend you rarely see: none but
those you usually pass and nod to.

Who will remember today at all, other than
how ordinary it was:
surely the water rests in the cove
and dandelions in bloom and in seed
blend with any other green day.

We remember well what we attend to well,
or when novelty or fear stuns.

—That heron's stillness *had* startled you still.
Its alertness flowed into your mind—

II.
Today, did you remember again: "He abused me,
he beat me, he defeated me,
he robbed me"?[2]

Or maybe you forgot before forgiving
or forgave before hearing
amends or even asking for them.

If you encounter your assailant again
on these winding paths around the cove,
will you remember the time you wished for his healing,
the width and screech of your heart as you yearned to protect
a world he might continue to harm?

---

[2] Buddha, *Dhammapada*, trans. F. Max Muller

Finally, deep upon the breath, you wish
for him, that he might know the peace
of not wanting to harm anyone.

You wish for him to feel how you felt
when *ahimsa* settled in—
after the fear shuddered awake and flew,
how the shock melted free
and you came home
to your body, to love, to this life,
today.

In fact, today, though the lilacs' flower heads have shriveled brown,
the dogwoods still bloom,
and as we walk, tulip tree blossoms
begin to fall
to the ground.

Transcendence/immanence

I have tasted transcendence—
beyond a holy love, or merging of two souls—
I held infinity, a few moments at a time.

Ordinary life afterwards seemed to be missing
some essential element.
My meditation lately has been to accept
a littler, more circumscribed life.
Seeking that bliss again only makes my
heart sore, like craving an unrequited love,
where devotion itself is almost enough to salve the pain it creates
but not quite.

Trouble is, a habit of loss turns into a habit of fear
and if we're not careful
the desire for communion becomes
a barrier to it.

Again and again I return to my meditation:
to open my heart to the little gifts,
to the mixed pleasures, to what is.

Today there was a light on the grass
for half a moment,
and it meant something—something about
spirit and body,
about what dies with the body
and what may live on with some kind of soul—
The glint, the green flashed an immanence,
and yet it said: no tool
of the mind is sharp enough
to cleave body and soul now,
conceptually, before the fact
of death,

it meant: trying to cleave will elude me,
will be more frustrating, more futile
than sheering passion from love.

All I will be left with is a cleaver,
glinting, flashing, same as the grass.

To be one of wisdom's guests

I wanted to be invited in
but all I could do
was peruse the grain of the door,
draw fingertips across the glow of the wood
in the many different lights
of the passing days.

Would age bring me in
passively, inevitably?
Would hard work open wisdom's door?
Would I ever? I am right here, at the stoop,
after all, and seem ready.

Then waiting,
patience turns from attentiveness
toward the ten thousand things:
the mulberry bushes outside
(who told me they were spiritual medicine?)
and the wisteria framing the door
(isn't love of beauty a path?)
In fact, I make a habit of a haphazard study
    of the infinite paths
to this threshold, where I keep
forgetting why I am here.
And the knocking turns to silence
turns to knocking
and finally, I turn back
to silence.

[coda] Touching the Earth
in gratitude for my sangha

Earth, my witness,
please tell me what you have seen.
I remember only parts of this life
and even less of others.

(I touch the earth
in tiny emulation.)

(Nothing quakes but
as I shift my spine
hands splay open
—whole body electric—
and the bell resounds.)

Feet touch earth: we walk.

Mist glides above the lake
like geese about to land;
ripples make water look
like it is moving as fast,
but that is just the surface,
just the eyes that see.

A new thought arises,
made of pieces of old thoughts,
and something wonders how thoughts form.
Who chooses of the vast store of consciousness,
infinite paint box, spectra
of light seen and unseen,
what will surface?

Earth, our witness,
please tell us what you see.
We are listening now.

As an environmental activist, **Karina Lutz** helped secure passage of sustainable energy legislation, thwart a proposed megaport, and restore wetlands in her home watershed of Narragansett Bay, RI. After receiving an MSJ from Medill School of Journalism, she worked as an editor, reporter, magazine publisher, and in nonprofit communications. She's currently collaborating to launch a permaculture community, Listening Tree Cooperative. She teaches yoga, sustainability, and deep ecology, and is poetry editor of *Deep Times: A Journal of the Work that Reconnects*.

Her poems have been published by Dark Mountain Project, *Tulane Review, Blueline, The Wayfarer, Twisted Vine, About Place Journal, Visitant*, Arachne Press, *Sediments, the RavensPerch, Clade Song, Miracle Monocle*, and *The Transnational*. She was semi-finalist in the Digging Press chapbook contest, received honorable mention for Homebound Poetry Prize twice, and in 2019 won the Landmark Prize for Fiction.

She studies body-mind therapies, herbs, permaculture, and the conscience/consensus nexus.

Her writing blog is at *karinautz.wordpress.com*. Her second book, *Preliminary Visions*, is forthcoming from Homebound Publications.

CPSIA information can be obtained
at www.ICGtesting.com
Printed in the USA
BVHW031206061220
595043BV00013B/784

9 781646 620647